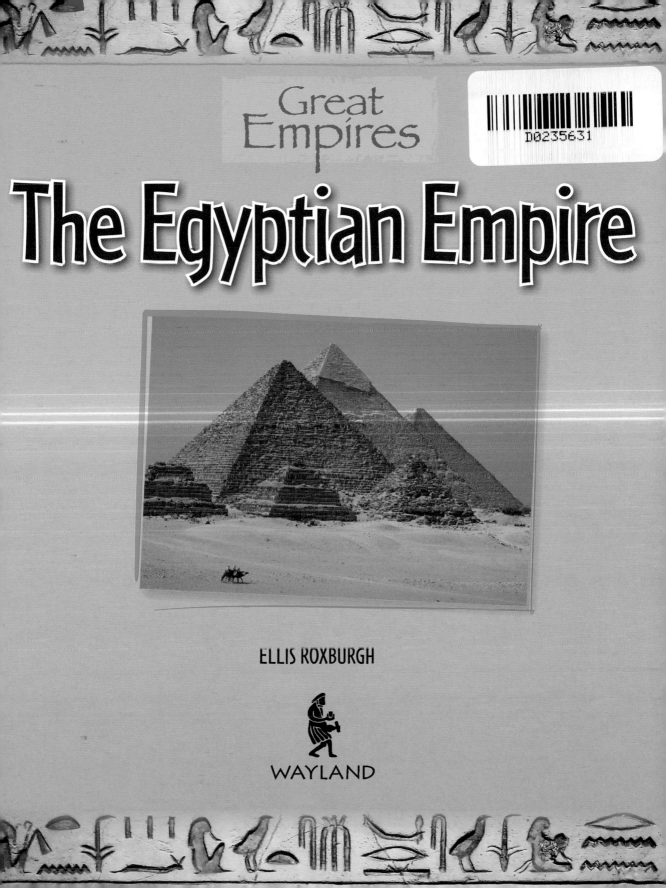

Great Empires

The Egyptian Empire

ELLIS ROXBURGH

WAYLAND

WAYLAND

www.waylandbooks.co.uk

First published in Great Britain in 2015 by Wayland

Copyright © 2015 Brown Bear Books Ltd

Wayland
An imprint of Hachette Children's Group
Part of Hodder & Stoughton
Carmelite House
50 Victoria Embankment
London EC4Y 0DZ
An Hachette UK Company
www.hachette.co.uk
www.hachettechildrens.co.uk

All Rights Reserved

Dewy number: 909'.0971232-dc23
ISBN: 978 0 7502 9662 5
10 9 8 7 6 5 4 3 2 1

Brown Bear Books Ltd
First Floor
9–17 St Albans Place
London
N1 0NX

Editorial Director: Lindsey Lowe
Managing Editor: Tim Cooke
Children's Publisher: Anne O'Daly
Design Manager: Keith Davis
Designer: Melissa Roskell
Picture Manager: Sophie Mortimer
Production Director: Alastair Gourlay

Printed in China

CONTENTS

Introduction

The Egyptian Empire reached its height in the 15th century BCE after a history lasting many centuries.

For the Egyptians of the New Kingdom, which lasted from about 1550 to 1070 BCE, the ancestors who built the famous pyramids at Giza were already figures of the distant past. The oldest pyramids were already nearly a thousand years old.

The temple at Abu Simbel was constructed by King Ramesses II to celebrate a military victory over the neighbouring Hittites.

The New Kingdom king Tutankhamun was buried with a gold death mask. The discovery of his tomb in 1922 made him one of the most famous Egyptian rulers.

The Egyptian civilisation grew up along the banks of the Nile River. The main settlements lay in the river's valley or in the broad delta, where the river divided into many waterways that flowed to the sea. The Egyptians depended on the river's annual flood, which covered the fields with fertile silt for growing crops. The river was also the main highway in a kingdom with few roads. Egypt was bordered by deserts that protected it from invasion.

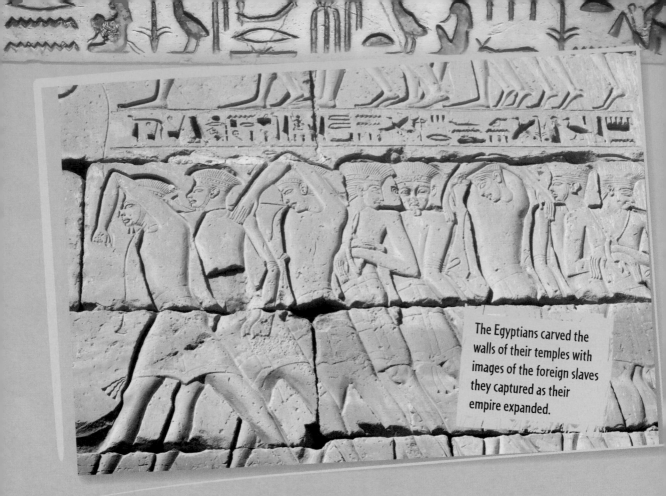

The Egyptians carved the walls of their temples with images of the foreign slaves they captured as their empire expanded.

Egyptian history is divided into three main periods: the Old Kingdom (2575–2134 BCE), the Middle Kingdom (2040–1640 BCE) and the New Kingdom (1550–1070 BCE). Between the kingdoms were times of upheaval known as the First and Second Intermediate periods. The kingdoms and intermediate periods are divided into **dynasties**, when they were ruled by members of the same family.

An Expanded Empire

This book is about the New Kingdom, when Egypt's armies began campaigns of conquest in search of resources, such as wood or gold. The armies pushed the frontiers of the empire further than ever.

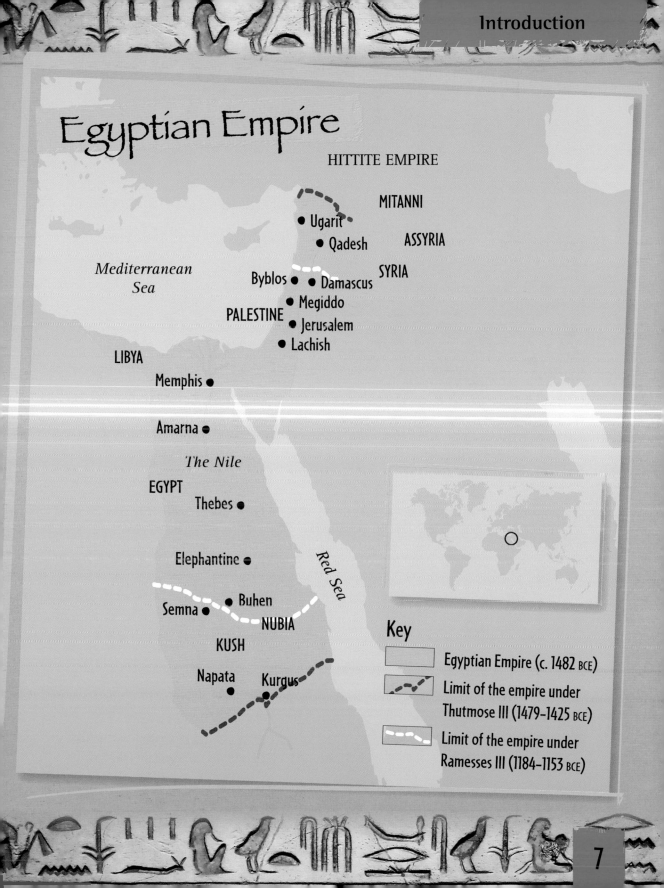

Egyptian Empire

HITTITE EMPIRE

MITANNI

● Ugarit

● Qadesh

ASSYRIA

Mediterranean Sea

Byblos ● ● Damascus

SYRIA

● Megiddo

PALESTINE

● Jerusalem

● Lachish

LIBYA

Memphis ●

Amarna ●

The Nile

EGYPT

Thebes ●

Elephantine ●

Red Sea

● Buhen

Semna ●

NUBIA

KUSH

Napata ●

Kurgus ●

Key

Egyptian Empire (c. 1482 BCE)

Limit of the empire under Thutmose III (1479–1425 BCE)

Limit of the empire under Ramesses III (1184–1153 BCE)

The Roots of the Empire

The civilisation of Egypt was already ancient when the period known as the New Kingdom began. The kings of the New Kingdom built an empire in north-east Africa and the Middle East.

By around 3000 BCE, small settlements had grown up along the banks of the Nile River, which was the lifeblood of Egypt. Tribal chiefs in southern Egypt (known as Upper Egypt) conquered the north (Lower Egypt), and the country was unified under the king, Narmer.

Pyramid Builders

Narmer founded the first of Egypt's dynasties of rulers. The kings had absolute authority in Egypt. The king was seen as the earthly representative of Egypt's many gods, and was the link between them and his subjects.

During the period known as the Old Kingdom (2575–2134 BCE), the kings built huge stone pyramids as tombs. The skills required to design and build the pyramids suggest the Egyptians had a high degree of scientific knowledge. Cutting the huge stone blocks, transporting them by

The Great Sphinx, a giant statue with a lion's body and a man's head, was carved in the desert near the Great Pyramids of Giza.

river and assembling them also suggest an advanced level of social organisation. The government coordinated vast numbers of builders to provide labour.

Old Kingdom Egypt was centralised. The king took responsibility for feeding his subjects. In exchange, his subjects worked for the state, growing crops or working on large-scale building projects.

By the 6th Dynasty, local rulers began to seize power in their own areas. They challenged and eventually destroyed the absolute power of the king. From 2134 BCE, Egypt experienced a period of instability and social unrest known as the First Intermediate Period.

The Middle Kingdom

Stability returned with the start of the Middle Kingdom in 2040 BCE. Egypt was reunited when Nebhepetre Mentuhotep II came to the throne

The Mystery of the Pyramids

The oldest pyramids were built over 4,500 years ago. They were built as burial chambers for the Egyptian kings of the Old Kingdom, but how they were built remains a mystery. King Khufu's Great Pyramid at Giza contains more than 2.3 million limestone blocks, some of which weigh 15 tonnes (14.75 tons). How the builders got these huge blocks into position was also a puzzle for the Egyptians of the New Kingdom. By then, the pyramids were already ancient.

The Great Pyramids of Giza were built during the Old Kingdom. They remained the tallest structures on Earth until the late 19th century.

A strip of vegetation marks an **oasis**, where an underground water supply reaches the surface of the desert.

Egypt's Landscape

Barren desert accounts for more than 90 per cent of Egypt. With almost no rainfall, the desert is known as the 'red land' and can support only small numbers of people near **wadis**, or seasonal streams, and oases. For the ancient Egyptians, the desert was both hostile and protective. It provided a formidable barrier against neighbouring countries and invading armies.

in the southern city of Thebes. He spent the first part of his reign conquering the kingdoms of northern Egypt and then became the ruler of a reunified country. Mentuhotep also built a **mausoleum** for himself to the west of Thebes, although it was not as impressive as the pyramids of the Old Kingdom rulers.

The Middle Kingdom brought four centuries of stability and prosperity, during which time Egypt traded with its neighbours. King Amenemhet III (ruled c.1860–1814 BCE) built himself two impressive pyramid complexes. After Amenemhet's death, however, some 70 kings ruled in just 150 years. Despite the

succession of short reigns, Egypt remained stable until around 1640 BCE, when a foreign people called the Hyksos took control of the north. Egypt fell into a period of instability, which is known as the Second Intermediate Period.

The Hyksos Period

The Hyksos formed the 15th Dynasty in Lower Egypt. At the same time, the 17th Dynasty, made up of native Egyptians, ruled Upper Egypt from their religious capital at Thebes. They were **vassals** of the Hyksos, meaning that they had to acknowledge the authority of the Hyksos. They also gave the Hyksos an annual amount of money and other goods, known as **tribute**.

On this side of the Narmer **Palette**, the king is about to strike a prisoner with a mace. Narmer wears the crown of Upper Egypt.

The Narmer Palette

The Narmer Palette is a shield-shaped stone that dates from about the 31st century BCE. Its significance lies in the images engraved on both sides. One side shows a king wearing the white crown of Upper Egypt. The other shows him wearing the red crown of Lower Egypt. Historians think the palette shows Narmer, who united Upper and Lower Egypt. It is the world's first-known document recording a historical event.

The Nile River

People could live in Egypt only because of the Nile River. People settled on the riverbanks, where the soil was made fertile by the rich silt left by the river's annual flooding. The river valley and delta were known as the 'black land' because of the colour of the silt (the desert was the 'red land'). The Nile was also Egypt's major highway. It was used to transport people and goods throughout the empire.

Expulsion of the Hyksos

Around 1550 BCE, the last king of the 17th Dynasty, Kamose, launched a war against the Hyksos to try to drive them out of Egypt. His armies reached the Hyksos capital of Avaris but did not conquer it. That job was left to Kamose's younger brother Ahmose (ruled 1550–1525 BCE).

Ships sailed on the Nile as far upstream as the First **Cataract**, where rapids made navigation difficult and risky.

This wall painting from a 19th-century BCE tomb is said to show the Hyksos people arriving in Egypt.

Ahmose drove the Hyksos out of Egypt. He also brought the whole country back together under a single ruler, and founded both the 18th Dynasty and the New Kingdom (1550–1070 BCE).

The New Kingdom

During the New Kingdom the most powerful of all the ancient Egyptian kingdoms emerged, and the Egyptian Empire spread to its greatest extent.

With Egypt free from its foreign rulers, Ahmose strengthened the army. He began a campaign to defeat and conquer Egypt's near neighbours to the north and south. This policy had two advantages. First, it safeguarded Egyptian territory from attack by other powers. Second, it gave Egypt access to a guaranteed supply of valuable resources that it lacked, but which its neighbours possessed.

KEY PEOPLE

The Hyksos

The Hyksos were most likely a group of immigrants from Syria-Palestine who moved into Lower Egypt. During a period of weak central government, they seized control of Lower Egypt with a minimum amount of warfare. They chose one of their own people as king rather than an Egyptian, but they did adopt some parts of old Egyptian culture. They used Egyptian royal dress and titles and continued to worship the sun god Re.

Building the Empire

After the reunification of Egypt, its rulers became ambitious to expand its power. They began campaigns of conquest to the south in Nubia and north along the eastern coast of the Mediterranean.

Statues of kings stand in a New Kingdom temple at Karnak. Amenhotep I made Karnak the centre of the new **cult** of Amun.

King Ahmose was the first Egyptian king in more than a century to build monuments in both Upper and Lower Egypt. This was a sign that the country was reunited. After he expelled the Hyksos, Ahmose continued fighting. He invaded Palestine (present-day Israel) to the north, where the Hyksos might have had **allies**. He also invaded Nubia in the south. By the end of his reign, Egypt was unified and financially stable. The Egyptian Empire was the major power of the region.

The Empire Consolidates

Ahmose's son, Amenhotep I (ruled 1525–1504 BCE), extended the empire further with successful conquests in Nubia. He also established features that would define the 18th Dynasty. He began the worship of the god Amun at Karnak, and he put all power in the hands of his own royal family. That prevented any other claims to the throne.

The Valley of the Kings is home to 63 royal tombs carved into the rocks. Twenty-six rulers are buried there.

Amenhotep's reign was largely peaceful. The king concentrated on opening mines and other economic activities. He carried on the programme of monument building. A special builders' village was founded at Deir el-Medina (see box, page 17).

Military Exploits

Amenhotep's heir, Thutmose I (ruled 1504–1492 BCE), was a relative by marriage and not a direct heir. He led expeditions into Syria and opened new territory for the empire. His army reached

Before the New Kingdom, the First Cataract at Aswan marked the southern boundary of Egyptian territory.

The Cataracts

The 6,853-kilometre (4,258-mile) course of the Nile is broken up by a series of six stretches of rapids known as cataracts. Ancient Egypt stretched south from the Nile Delta to the First Cataract at Aswan. Five more cataracts lay south of Aswan. The shallow waters are full of boulders and rocks. They prevent ships from navigating the whole length of the river.

the Euphrates River in the north and the Fourth Cataract (rapids) in the south. Egypt became even more powerful in the region. Syria and Palestine were required to pay tribute to Egypt, and their rulers swore allegiance to the Egyptian king. Nubia, meanwhile, became an Egyptian **colony**. It was valuable because of its gold. Nubia was ruled by a **viceroy** sent to Nubia by the Egyptian king.

To maintain control, Egypt now had a permanent army. In times of peace, the soldiers worked on building projects. They were called to go into Nubia during the brief reign of Thutmose II (ruled 1492–

1479 BCE) to put down uprisings. Thutmose is best known for his wife and half-sister, Hatshepsut. She ruled Egypt for 20 years as **regent** for her stepson, Thutmose III, who was too young to take the throne when his father died.

A Female 'King'

Hatshepsut (regent 1479–c. 1459 BCE) was known as a 'king' rather than a queen. Her 20-year reign was one of the most successful of the 18th Dynasty. She was a capable and bold leader, and also began an ambitious building programme. She built a **mortuary temple** for herself at Deir el-Bahri.

DAILY LIFE

Deir el-Medina

The kings of the 18th Dynasty made the bank across from Thebes the site of their royal tombs. The construction of what is now called the Valley of the Kings required a huge workforce. To house the workers, Thutmose I created the village of Deir el-Medina near the tombs. The workers who lived there enjoyed privileges, such as generous food rations.

These pottery storage jars, known as amphoras, were discovered by archaeologists working at the site of Deir el-Medina.

Female Rulers

Hatshepsut was not the only female ruler in ancient Egypt. Women often ruled as regents until their sons came of age. Other examples include Sobekneferu of the 12th Dynasty (ruled 1777–1773 BCE). In the 1st century BCE, Cleopatra was the last ruler of ancient Egypt. There was no **hieroglyph** for 'queen', so female rulers were given the title of 'king'. Hatshepsut took her role as king so seriously that she was portrayed as a man, with a false beard.

Hatshepsut intended her temple to be a fitting memorial to her position as ruler and wife of the god Amun. She also changed the appearance of the religious centres of Thebes and Karnak with her building programme of temples, tombs and four-sided, pyramid-topped columns.

Unlike her predecessors, Hatshepsut did not go to war with Egypt's neighbours in order to expand the empire. She did, however, ensure that Nubia remained an Egyptian colony. She sent the army to put down uprisings there and encouraged trade in Nubia's precious resources.

This kneeling statue of Hatshepsut was one of a number that once lined an avenue. The queen is shown with a king's false beard.

Hatshepsut was buried in the mortuary temple she built for herself, one of the most spectacular of all Egyptian buildings.

Trade Mission to Punt

Hatshepsut was eager to strengthen her position as a woman in a man's role. One way she did this was by following the actions of earlier kings, such as sending trade missions to distant lands. Hatshepsut sent a mission to Punt in the ninth year of her rule. Punt probably lay near the Red Sea, although its location is not certain. It was a source of prized luxury goods. Hatshepsut's ships returned loaded with incense, myrrh, ivory, ebony, leopard skins and gold. The success of the mission sealed Hatshepsut's position as king.

Hatshepsut ruled for around 20 years before Thutmose III took the throne. She had probably died, although she may have simply moved aside.

KEY PEOPLE

Senenmut

During the New Kingdom, royal officials held great power. Senenmut served Hatshepsut in high-ranking roles, including as chancellor and as tutor to her daughter. His importance is clear from the many statues of him that have been recovered: 26 so far. Some historians maintain that the existence of so many statues suggests that Senenmut was actually Hatshepsut's partner.

The Height of the Empire

When Thutmose III finally assumed the throne from his stepmother Hatshepsut, Egypt was in a strong position. The new king took advantage of that strength.

Thutmose III (ruled 1479–1425 BCE, including Hatshepsut's regency) was an aggressive leader. He was determined to cement Egypt's position and to increase its territories by waging war. He added to the gains made by Thutmose I and Amenhotep II. His success was due mainly to the large size of the Egyptian army and to the skill of its generals.

Battle of Megiddo

Thutmose III's first military goal was to capture Megiddo, in what is now Israel. The city fought against Egyptian domination. Although Thutmose easily surrounded the city, Megiddo was hard to conquer and fell only after a seven-month siege.

Thutmose III then fought another 17 military campaigns as he tried to take control of the Syria–Palestine region. As he captured state after state, he installed local rulers to govern on his behalf.

Thutmose III came to the throne in his own right in 1459 BCE and began a series of campaigns to increase Egyptian power.

This painting from a wall of the tomb of Hatshepsut shows Egyptian soldiers armed with spears and carrying long shields.

To make sure they remained loyal, he took their brothers and children back to Egypt and kept them as hostages.

Thutmose III campaigned further than any other Egyptian king. The Egyptian Empire reached its maximum extent. It stretched from the bend in the Euphrates River near Karkamish, 1,400 kilometres (870 miles) north of Thebes, to the Fourth Cataract over 1,000 kilometres (620 miles) south of Thebes. Egyptian control was strong in the south in Nubia and Kush, but in the north it was fragile. Thutmose put a lot of effort into keeping hold of Syria–Palestine. No Egyptian king would ever again control as much territory.

KEY PEOPLE

The Egyptian Army

During the 18th Dynasty, the army became a powerful force in Egypt. It was well organised, with the king in overall command and separate divisions of infantry and cavalry. Both divisions were divided into groups of 50 men led by an officer. In peacetime, soldiers worked on civil projects such as digging **irrigation** canals or moving stones for construction projects.

The Great Hypostyle Hall of the Temple of Amun at Karnak was built by kings of the 19th Dynasty on a design begun by Hatshepsut.

BELIEFS

Amun

During the New Kingdom, Amun was the most important of Egypt's hundreds of **deities**. He was the sun god, known as Amun-Re, the giver of all life, and he also took other forms. He protected the king when he went into battle. Amun's position was challenged briefly when Akhenaten replaced him with another sun god, Aten.

Thutmose III took his son, Amenhotep II (ruled 1425–1401 BCE), as his heir. Amenhotep's long reign was followed by that of Thutmose IV (ruled 1401–1391 BCE), who continued to fight in the Syria–Palestine region.

Amenhotep III

The 38-year reign of Amenhotep III (ruled 1391–1353 BCE) was different from those of his predecessors. The king did not lead his own army, instead sending his generals to war on his behalf. Amenhotep concentrated on building structures that reflected the power of the Egyptian Empire. He added to the temple of the god

Amun at Karnak and built a temple to the god of war, Montu. This might indicate how important war had become to the 18th Dynasty as a way of expanding its territory and earning revenue in the form of slaves and booty. The conquered lands provided a supply of tribute. Mercenaries and foreigners boosted the ranks of the Egyptian army. The towns and cities that lined the banks of the Nile were full of shrines, temples and monuments dedicated to Amun. What happened next was unexpected.

An Unusual King

Akhenaten (ruled 1353–1335 BCE) took over the throne from Amenhotep III, his father. He broke with the traditions of the 18th Dynasty. Amenhotep's devotion to the cult of Amun, the sun god, had made the priests of Amun rich and powerful. Akhenaten wanted to weaken their

KEY PEOPLE

Akhenaten

Akhenaten was probably the most unusual of all the Egyptian kings. His decision to make Aten the sole god of the Egyptians is the earliest example of monotheism, or the worship of a single god. Today, monotheism is widespread: Christianity, Judaism and Islam have a single god. The Egyptians, however, resented the abandonment of their hundreds of other gods. Akhenaten's new religion lasted for only 20 years. After his death, the old gods were restored.

Statues and paintings of Akhenaten show him in a more realistic way than the usual stylised images of Egyptian kings.

position, so he banned the worship of Amun. In his place he put a new god, Aten. Aten was not just a new sun god. He was to be the only god in Egypt. Akhenaten built shrines and temples to Aten and ordered the destruction and defacing of the temples dedicated to Amun and the many other gods. He also moved the capital from Thebes to a new city named El-Amarna.

Amarna Letters

The Amarna Letters are a collection of 382 documents that record Egypt's relations with its neighbours. The clay tablets were inscribed with **cuneiform** writing during a 15- to 30-year period. The tablets were discovered in 1887 at the site of Akhenaten's capital city. They record correspondence between Egyptian and neighbouring rulers and from Egypt to its **diplomats** in Canaan and Amurru. The letters were written in Akkadian, which was the diplomatic language of Mesopotamia.

Although he was busy with the worship of Aten, Akhenaten continued to wage war against his subjects who opposed Egyptian authority. He had military success in Kush, but he did not have the political skills to deal with the ongoing unrest in Syria–Palestine. The empire started to unravel. Although Akhenaten was very unpopular with the priests and the army because of his devotion to Aten, he was not overthrown as king. He died peacefully in the 17th year of his reign.

The Old Order Restored

Akhenaten's son, Tutankhamun (ruled 1333–1323 BCE) was just 10 years old when his father died. With no immediate family to rule as regents, officials ruled for the king and set about restoring the old order. Amun was restored to his position as chief god and the capital city was moved to Memphis, which had been the capital of the 1st to the 8th dynasties of the Old Kingdom. However, Tutankhamun did not live long enough to make a huge impact. He died aged about 19. He is remembered today mainly because of his tomb and its treasures, which were discovered in 1922.

The 19th Dynasty

With the death of Tutankhamun, the 18th Dynasty was effectively over. An army officer named Horemheb (ruled 1319–1292 BCE) declared himself king. When he died, his deputy, Paramessu, became king and changed his name to Ramesses I

This carved pillar stood in a temple built to Hathor in the Sinai Peninsula, a desert region where the Egyptians mined turquoise.

KEY PEOPLE

Nefertiti

Thanks to the famous bust in Berlin's Neues Museum, Nefertiti (c. 1370–c. 1330 BCE) has one of the most recognisable faces in the world. The chief wife of Akhenaten, Nefertiti joined her husband in the worship of just one god, Aten. Like Akhenaten, she was portrayed in a remarkably realistic style. Some historians think that Nefertiti might have ruled Egypt briefly after her husband's death, but this has never been proved.

This carving on a temple wall shows Egyptian soldiers using ladders to climb the walls of Qadesh to attack the Hittites.

Tutankhamun's Death

The treasures found in Tutankhamun's tomb and his death at around age 19 led to all kinds of speculation that he was murdered. Scientists have used advances in **DNA** analysis and **forensic** pathology to investigate his body. It now seems more likely that he died from a disease. It might have been a genetic condition because his royal parents were brother and sister.

(ruled 1292–1290 BCE). Ramesses is seen as the founder of the 19th Dynasty, even though he ruled for only 18 months. His son, Seti I (ruled 1290–1279 BCE), was determined to regain territory Egypt had lost in Syria and Palestine. A new power had emerged in the north, the Hittites. They drove the Egyptians from the region.

Ramesses II

Seti I named his son, Ramesses II, as co-ruler. By the time Seti died, Ramesses was experienced at government. His long and stable reign (1279–1213 BCE) saw Egypt restore its military prowess. Ramesses was determined to retake Syria–Palestine from the Hittites. In 1274 BCE, he led his

Obelisks

Among the most common Egyptian monuments were obelisks. These tall, four-sided carved pillars tapered into a pyramid at their tops. Usually carved from a single piece of stone, the obelisks were decorated with hieroglyphs with the titles of kings and dedications to gods. The obelisks were placed in pairs at the entrances of temples. Today, ancient Egyptian obelisks stand in major cities around the world.

army north. They clashed with the Hittites in the Battle of Qadesh. Although Ramesses seemed to have been outmanoeuvred by the Hittite general Muwattallis, the Egyptians avoided defeat. The Egyptian army withdrew south, but Ramesses vowed to get his revenge. Four years later, Ramesses marched north again and won some victories, but his territorial gains were temporary. The Hittites regained control as soon as the Egyptian army left.

Eventually, Ramesses II gave up fighting in Syria. Instead, he turned his attention to a huge building programme that included the great temples at Karnak, Abydos and Abu Simbel. By the time Ramesses II died, he was probably around 92 years of age. He left a huge legacy of monuments, obelisks and statues. He was buried in the Valley of the Kings.

A carved head of Ramesses II lies in front of a row of statues in a courtyard of his mortuary temple, the Ramesseum in Luxor.

The Peoples of the Empire

Immediately before the New Kingdom started with the 18th Dynasty in 1550, foreigners known as the Hyksos ruled Egypt. Later, the Egyptians came to rule some of their neighbours.

Egypt lay at a geographical crossroads where several regions met. The Nile River attracted settlers and travellers. The Egyptians had a history of interacting with their neighbours. Sometimes the Egyptians ruled others; at other times, they were ruled by foreigners.

The Hyksos

The rulers of the 15th Dynasty were foreigners. The Hyksos had arrived from Palestine and settled in the Nile Delta. This multiracial people dominated Egypt for over a century during the Second Intermediate Period.

This New Kingdom tomb painting shows captured Nubians, who were highly valued as slaves in Egypt.

In this wall carving, Hittites are shown being crushed beneath the wheels of an Egyptian chariot during a battle.

The Hyksos had a lasting effect on Egypt thanks to the technical expertise and weapons they introduced. They brought knowledge of bronze-working to Egypt, and their farmers introduced new crops and new animals. The Hyksos also introduced the horse and the two-wheeled chariot, which Egyptian armies adopted. The weapons introduced by the Hyksos – the composite bow and the battleaxe also proved decisive in Egypt's expansion during the New Kingdom.

The Nubians

The kingdom of Nubia (present-day Sudan) lay south of Egypt. Nubia's culture was much older than Egypt's. The ancient

Egyptian Snobs

The Egyptians saw themselves as being superior to all other peoples. In their art, they either depicted foreigners as prisoners or showed them paying tribute to Egypt's rulers. They pictured the Nubians from the south, the Libyans from the west and the 'vile Asiatics' from the east on the king's footstools or on the soles of his sandals. When the king walked, it symbolised Egypt trampling on its neighbours.

An Egyptian soldier captures Hittite prisoners in this carving from the temple of Ramesses II.

DAILY LIFE

Byblos

The present-day town of Byblos on the Mediterranean coast of what is now Lebanon was once an important trading port for the Egyptians. From the time of the unification of Upper and Lower Egypt, it was a source of timber. The Egyptians prized the famous cedars of Lebanon for their building projects because the trees were very tall, straight and strong. Merchants shipped the timber from Byblos back to Egypt.

Nubian language is the oldest-known language in Africa. The Egyptians made frequent attacks on Nubia to seize slaves and natural resources such as gold. Later, they seized Nubian territory south of Aswan and took it into the empire as the province of Upper Egypt. The Nubian men were known for their horsemanship and archery skills, and were used in the Egyptian army's cavalry division.

The Hittites

Far to the north of Egypt – more than 965 kilometres (600 miles) away – was the Hittite Empire of what is now Turkey. The Hittites were a warlike people. The

Egyptians tried repeatedly to take territory from them in Syria–Palestine but had little lasting success. The Hittites, like the Hyksos, were skilled chariot builders. They used chariots to great effect against the Egyptian armies. The Egyptians learnt various skills from the Hittites, such as iron-working. The Hittites had, in turn, learnt many of their skills, including cuneiform writing, from the Mesopotamians. The Egyptians adopted cuneiform writing for their diplomatic letters.

The Kingdom of Kush

After the New Kingdom collapsed around 1070 BCE, Egypt entered another phase of instability. Nubia broke free of its colonial ruler and became the Kingdom of Kush.

In the 8th century BCE, King Kashta of Kush invaded a weakened Egypt, and the Kushian kings became the pharaohs (rulers) of the 25th Dynasty. They controlled Egypt until 656 BCE. Unlike the Egyptians, the Kushians buried their rulers in mass graves alongside their faithful advisers.

KEY PEOPLE

The Sea Peoples

During the 19th Dynasty, tribes from the north known as the Sea Peoples – so called because they travelled by boat – began to arrive in Egypt. Archaeologists think they were driven south by famine and planned to settle in Egypt rather than simply invade. Wall paintings show them not as warriors but as families with all their possessions.

This carving shows the profile of an official in the court of Assyria, a kingdom north-east of Egypt in what is now Iraq.

Life in the Empire

For Egyptians of the New Kingdom, life was stable and organised. Everyone knew their place and their job. The state controlled most aspects of their lives.

The king, or pharaoh, was at the head of Egyptian society. He was seen as a god and the son of Amun, the sun god. The pharaoh owned all of Egypt: its land, natural resources and trade with other peoples. The pharaoh was assisted by a **vizier**, or chief official, who controlled the officials who ran Egypt. Many of these officials were members of the extended royal family. That helped ensure none of them would challenge the pharaoh's position.

Beneath the officials in the social ladder were the craftworkers. Their jobs were handed from father to son. They were masons, sculptors, painters, carpenters, goldsmiths, leather-workers, chariot-builders and weapon-makers. Lower down the social scale were brickmakers and potters.

Colossal statues of pharaohs, like this one of Ramesses II, reminded Egyptians of the god-like status of their rulers.

A boy began learning his father's trade at age five, while girls were brought up to help their mothers in the home. Some boys trained to become scribes. Most Egyptians were unable to read or write, so being a scribe was an important job. Scribes belonged to the class of officials and were well paid. After attending school for several years, a boy could become a junior scribe at age 12.

At the bottom of the social ladder were slaves. They were often foreigners captured during war, and the many battles of the New Kingdom saw a huge rise in the numbers of slaves in Egypt. The slaves worked in the fields and on the many massive building projects that were a feature of the New Kingdom.

The Yearly Flood

The basis of Egypt's life and economy was the **inundation**, or the annual flooding of the Nile. Every June, the Nile began to rise until the water flooded over the banks and across the surrounding land. People along

Scribes learnt three different scripts: hieroglyphics for sacred writing, hieratic for less formal use and demotic for daily use.

Pharaoh or King?

The word 'pharaoh' originally meant 'great house' and referred to the royal palace. During Hatshepsut's reign (c. 1479-1458 BCE), the title began to be used to refer to the ruler - the female 'king' - rather than the building. After Hatshepsut's stepson Thutmose III became king, the title 'pharaoh' was widely used for the king, but also to refer to the son of Amun.

This detail from a tomb painting shows farmers with livestock, including goats and sheep.

the river had to travel by boat or on raised walkways. The flood started to subside in September and was over by November. Farmers then ploughed the nutrient-rich silt left by the flood into their fields to grow crops. They also used the floodwaters for irrigation. If the flood failed, famine followed because Egypt does not have enough rainfall to water crops.

Farming

Farmers used ploughs pulled by oxen or donkeys to plough the silt into their fields. They grew mainly barley and wheat, which were stored in royal **granaries** in case of later famine. Fruit, such as grapes, figs, apples, pomegranates and dates, and vegetables, such as lettuces, radishes, gourds and onions, grew easily in the rich soil. Farmers grew flax to turn into **linen** for clothing. Reeds were also used to make boats, ropes, mats, sandals and **papyrus**, which is a kind of paper.

Food and Drink

The Nile provided people with plenty of fish. Even poor families ate well. Although laws forbade Egyptians from catching the fish, these were widely ignored. Rich Egyptians ate beef, goat and lamb. Pigs were reserved for sacrifices to the gods, but some poor people ate pork. Wild birds

DAILY LIFE

The Shaduf

The shaduf was a hand-operated device used to lift water out of the Nile or canals to irrigate crops. A pole resting on a **fulcrum** had a bucket on a rope at one end and a weight on the other, shorter end. The farmer lowered the bucket to fill it with water, then used the weight to raise the bucket and pour the water onto the fields.

Farmers chop down trees and clear land ready for planting with crops in this detail from a wall painting.

The symbols in hieroglyphic writing could stand for words or sounds, depending on how they were used.

were hunted for food. Bread made from barley or wheat was a staple, and soldiers received a daily ration of bread. Everyone drank beer, made from barley. Date wine was popular and grape wine a rare treat.

Towns and Houses

Most Egyptian towns stood close to the Nile or a canal so that families could get fresh water. The houses were built from sun-dried mud bricks. Stone was used only in temples and other buildings owned by the pharaoh. The richer the family, the more storeys their home had. Poor families lived in two or three rooms on one floor, while an official's home could have two or even three storeys. The houses had flat roofs. People did their cooking on the roof. They also slept on the roof when it was too hot to stay inside.

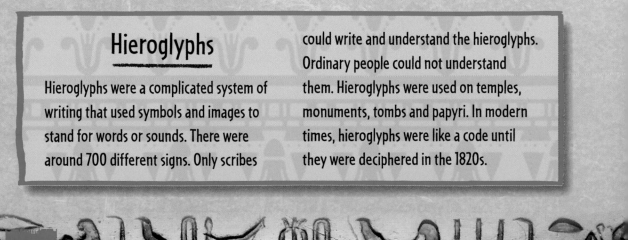

Hieroglyphs

Hieroglyphs were a complicated system of writing that used symbols and images to stand for words or sounds. There were around 700 different signs. Only scribes could write and understand the hieroglyphs. Ordinary people could not understand them. Hieroglyphs were used on temples, monuments, tombs and papyri. In modern times, hieroglyphs were like a code until they were deciphered in the 1820s.

Wealthy homes had gardens surrounded by high walls. The rooms were decorated with flower paintings, colourful rugs and furniture made from wood inlaid with gold, ivory and mother-of-pearl.

Clothing

The Egyptians needed few clothes because it was hot all year and there was virtually no rain. Even so, clothes were a good indication of a person's wealth. The richer the person, the finer the quality of linen they wore. Men wore plain kilts and sometimes a cape. New Kingdom women wore close-fitting, ankle-length tunics with fashionable narrow pleats. Jewellery was popular with men and women and both sexes wore make-up. Men were clean-shaven, although the pharaoh wore

Valley of the Kings

The kings of the New Kingdom made their religious capital in Thebes in Upper Egypt. They also established a new burial ground on the western side of the Nile in what is now called the Valley of the Kings. Unlike the pyramids of the Old Kingdom, these tombs were carved into the rock or hidden underground. This might have been to discourage robbers from stealing the funeral goods buried with the kings, which is what had happened to the goods in pyramids.

These ruins are the walls of the houses in Deir el-Medina, built to house the workers who constructed the tombs in the Valley of the Kings.

Treasures of the Tomb

The Egyptians believed in life after death, so they thought a dead person would need all their possessions to help them in their new life. For the kings, this meant burying them with magnificent treasure, often made from solid gold. Items might include weapons, clothes, furniture, jewellery, musical instruments and even full-sized boats. For ordinary people, the objects were simpler and made from cheaper materials.

a false ceremonial beard, together with the double crown of Upper and Lower Egypt. The pharaoh wore linen so fine it was almost transparent.

Religion and the Afterlife

Every part of daily life was controlled by a god. For most of the New Kingdom, the chief god was Amun, the sun god, but there were more than 600 gods and goddesses. Some deities were associated with a specific town, but others were important everywhere, including the falcon-headed Horus, who ruled the living, and Osiris, the god of the underworld.

The Egyptians believed the dead enjoyed an afterlife, or life after death. To be ready

This photograph shows piles of chests and pottery jars buried in the tomb of an official from the time of the New Kingdom.

for the afterlife, the body was preserved and buried with everything the person would need in the next life. As well as food and drink, this might include valuable possessions, animals and even servants who were buried with the dead person.

Leisure Time

Egyptian society was prosperous enough for people to have a lot of free time. Young children filled their time playing with toys. Older boys made up war games and girls enjoyed dancing. Adults played a game called senet, which was like an early form of chess. Men hunted and fished, although only the pharaoh was permitted to hunt in the desert.

The Egyptians wrapped mummies in layers of linen tape with lucky charms and decorative chestpieces, as seen here.

BELIEFS

Mummies

To enter the afterlife, an Egyptian body had to be preserved by being turned into a mummy. The mummification of a corpse took 70 days. First, the brain was pulled out through the nose and the organs were removed and stored in jars. The jars would be placed alongside the mummified body in the burial chamber. The body was dried in a salt called natron. It was then embalmed, washed and wrapped in layers of linen before it was placed in a wooden coffin inside a stone coffin.

Fall of the Empire

The reign of Ramesses II was the high point of the 19th Dynasty. The late New Kingdom was dominated by challenges that eventually weakened the power of the Egyptian kings.

During the 20th Dynasty, only the reigns of Ramesses III (ruled 1184–1153 BCE) and Ramesses IV (ruled 1153–1147 BCE) approached the heights of the reign of Ramesses II. There were many warning signs that the New Kingdom was in a serious decline.

Rise of the Amun Priest Cult

The biggest threat the later kings of the dynasty faced was the unstoppable rise in power of the Amun priests in Thebes. Previously, the king had owned all of Egypt's land. By the reign of Ramesses III, however, one-third of all farmland was

Ramesses III leads a procession of priests from Karnak. By the late New Kingdom, the king and priests were competing for power.

owned by the temples, three-quarters of which belonged to the Amun cult. This upset the balance of power within Egypt. It also caused an economic crisis in which grain prices soared. In the 29th year of Ramesses III's reign, the state was late paying food rations to the workers at Deir el-Medina. The workers put down their tools and refused to work until they were paid. It was the first recorded strike in history.

Invaders

With the priests of Amun holding more power, the king's power was reduced. The kings could still rely on the army for support, but there were now more battles to fight as Egypt was frequently invaded. One group of invaders was the Sea Peoples, a name that may describe people from Anatolia or Greece who moved around the

This statue of Amun stood in his temple at Karnak, which became the centre of the god's powerful cult.

KEY PEOPLE

Attempted Assassination

The Egyptians recorded that, near the end of his life, Ramesses III was the victim of a planned murder. Some women in his court plotted with court officials to murder the king during the annual Opet Festival in Thebes. They wanted to replace him with Pentaweret, who was the son of Tiy, one of Ramesses' wives. The records do not say what became of the plot, but scientific tests on Ramesses' mummy suggest that his throat was cut. Perhaps the plot succeeded.

This carving shows Ramesses II in his chariot fighting the Hittites at Qadesh. The battle was far closer than the Egyptians depicted.

Beefing It Up!

Many reliefs on temple walls show Egyptian battles in great detail. On temples at Abydos, Karnak and Abu Simbel, for example, the Battle of Qadesh fought by Rameses II against the Hittites is portrayed as a magnificent victory for the Egyptians. The depictions are misleading, however. In fact, the battle was not the clear victory the artists showed. The depictions belonged to a tradition in which rulers often exaggerated their achievements.

Mediterranean coast. They mounted raids on Egypt from the reign of Ramesses II, and grew bolder as they enjoyed military success elsewhere in the region.

Under Ramesses III, the Sea People destroyed the Hittite Empire to the north. They set their sights on Egypt, but the king pushed the invaders back. Such successes became rare, however, as Egypt grew weaker. In the remainder of the 20th Dynasty, Egypt lost control of Syria–Palestine to the north, while its hold on the colony in Nubia also weakened.

The Final Reigns

With the power struggle between king and priests, increasingly bold invaders and soaring grain prices, Egypt was engulfed by civil unrest. Under Ramesses IX (ruled 1126–1108 BCE), the viceroy of Nubia went to war with Amenhotep, high priest of Amun. Although Amenhotep was defeated, the civil war showed that the power of the central government had collapsed. As instability grew, robbers broke into the kings' tombs. It was a sign that the Egyptians had stopped seeing their kings as representatives of Amun.

When Ramesses XI (ruled 1099–1069 BCE) died, Egypt split. The priests of Amun took control of Middle and Upper Egypt. Control of Lower Egypt passed to the man who buried Ramesses XI, Smendes, who was not of royal birth. He founded the 21st Dynasty (1069–945 BCE).

KEY PEOPLE

Rise of the Priests

During the late New Kingdom, the power of Egyptian priests rose spectacularly. By the late 19th and 20th dynasties, two families, connected by marriage, controlled the Amun cult in Karnak. Although they could not become kings, they had great power. Eventually the high priest was shown in reliefs as having the same status as the king.

Ruined pyramids stand in Nubia. Nubia freed itself from Egyptian control and a Nubian dynasty later came to rule Egypt.

Timeline

2575 BCE   Beginning of the Old Kingdom in Egypt.

2134 BCE   Beginning of a period of instability in the First Intermediate Period.

2040 BCE   The Middle Kingdom marks the beginning of another period of peace.

c. 1640 BCE   The arrival of the Hyksos in the Nile Delta marks the start of the Second Intermediate Period.

1550 BCE   Kamose, the last king of the 17th Dynasty, goes to war with the Hyksos. His brother, Ahmose, comes to the throne and completes the defeat of the Hyksos, reuniting Egypt. He is the founder of the 18th Dynasty and the New Kingdom.

1525 BCE   Amenhotep becomes king.

1504 BCE   Thutmose I becomes king.

1492 BCE   The throne passes to Thutmose II.

c. 1479 BCE   Hatshepsut becomes regent for her stepson and co-ruler, Thutmose III.

c. 1469 BCE   Hatshepsut sends a successful trade mission to Punt, an area thought to be near the Red Sea to the south-east of Egypt.

c. 1459 BCE   Thutmose III begins to rule in his own right. He soon defeats rebellious Canaanites in the Battle of Meggido, the first battle in history recorded in any detail.

1391 BCE   Amenhotep III becomes king.

1353 BCE   Akhenaten becomes king and brings in sweeping religious reforms, introducing the worship of a single god, Aten.

1333 BCE   Tutankhamun comes to the throne.

1323 BCE   Tutankhamun dies young and is buried in a tomb that will later become one of the most celebrated of all Egyptian treasures.

1319 BCE   A commoner and former army officer, Horemheb, comes to the throne and begins to overturn the religious reforms of Akhenaten.

1292 BCE   The vizier Paramessu comes to the throne and takes the name Ramesses I; he is the first ruler of the 19th Dynasty.

c. 1290 BCE   Seti I comes to the throne and expands the Egyptian Empire.

1279 BCE   Ramesses II becomes king. He will expand the empire to its greatest territorial extent.

c. 1274 BCE   Ramesses II fights the Hittites in the Battle of Qadesh.

1213 BCE   The death of Ramesses II marks the beginning of a rapid decline in the power of the Egyptian Empire.

1070 BCE   The New Kingdom collapses after a succession of weak leaders and the split of Egypt.

Glossary

allies States that cooperate to achieve a particular goal.

assassinate To murder someone for a political reason.

cataract A large waterfall or stretch of rough water.

colony A country that is fully controlled by another country.

cult A system of religious devotion based on a single god or person.

cuneiform A kind of writing made by pressing a wedge-shaped stylus into soft clay.

deity A god or goddess.

diplomat An official who represents his or her country abroad.

DNA Deoxyribonucleic acid, a material that passes on genetic information from parents to offspring.

dynasty A series of rulers who are members of the same family.

forensic Using scientific methods to investigate crimes.

fulcrum The support on which a lever rests.

granary A storehouse for keeping grain.

hieroglyphs A form of picture writing used in ancient Egypt.

inundation The annual flood of the Nile River.

irrigation The supply of water to crops.

linen A fine, soft textile made from the flax plant.

mausoleum A grand building holding a tomb or tombs.

mortuary temple A temple constructed next to a royal tomb.

oasis An isolated area of vegetation around a water source in a desert.

palette A thin slab used to mix paints, make-up or inks.

papyrus Paper-like sheets made from the stems of a water plant.

regent Someone who governs a country on behalf of a ruler, often because the ruler is too young.

tribute Payment made by one ruler to another.

vassal A country or person that is subordinate to another.

viceroy Someone who rules a colony on behalf of a monarch.

vizier A high official.

wadi A valley or channel that is dry except in the rainy season.

Further Reading

Books

Bingham, Jane, *Ancient Egyptians* (Explore!), Wayland, 2014.

Cooke, Tim, *The Ancient Egyptians* (At Home With), Wayland, 2014.

Ganeri, Anita, *Ancient Egypt* (Great Civilisations), Franklin Watts, 2014.

Glifford, Clive, *Ancient Egypt* (The Best and Worst Jobs), Wayland, 2015.

Minay, Rachel, *Ancient Egypt* (The History Detective Investigates), Wayland, 2014.

Steele, Philip, *Empires* (Epic!), Wayland, 2015.

Steele, Philip, *Explorers* (Epic!), Wayland, 2015.

Websites

Ancient Egypt – The British Museum
www.ancientegypt.co.uk

The British Museum's website about ancient Egypt, with many artifacts from the museum's collection.

BBC History
www.bbc.co.uk/history/ancient/egyptians

Pages about all aspects of ancient Egypt from BBC History (archived site).

Discovering Ancient Egypt
discoveringegypt.com

Pages about ancient Egyptian hieroglyphics, gods and kings, and 3D reconstructions of temples.

History on the Net
www.historyonthenet.com/egyptians/egyptiansmain.htm

History on the Net pages about life and society in ancient Egypt.

Index